Poems by James Den Boer

University of Pittsburgh Press

Library of Congress Catalog Card Number 78–134492
ISBN 0–8229–3216–4 (cloth)
ISBN 0–8229–5221–1 (paper)
Copyright © 1971, James Den Boer
All rights reserved
Henry M. Snyder & Co., Inc., London
Manufactured in the United States of America

Acknowledgment is made to the following journals in which some of these
poems first appeared: *Concerning Poetry, Dragonfly, Hill Record, Jeopardy,
New River, Northwest Review, Poetry Northwest, Spectacle,* and *Sumac.*

"Rock and Sea" was first published as a broadside by Graham Mackintosh,
the White Rabbit Press, San Francisco.

for
William H. Brown
and
Emily Cady Williams

*And that, knowing the
time, that now it is
high time to awake out
of sleep.*
         Rom. 13:11

CONTENTS

I

Our Own Water 3
Casting a Vote 4
Aiming at Birds 5
First Rains 7
The Garden 8
The Quail 10
Hoping for a New Life 14

II

Muttering 19

III

Typing 33
Part of a Week in Washington 34
Song 35
Moose Call 36
Old Country 37
Charming the Moon 38
The Bead Colors 39
America 41

IV

Mix 45
Here Are the Words 47
Rock and Sea 48
    Walking Toward the Sea 48
    A Strong Tide 49
    East Beach 50
    Riding by the Sea 51
    Rock and Sea 53
Trying to Come Apart 54

OUR OWN WATER

Our own water, from our own well,
hard, mineral, rusty—
turning on the tap just to taste it,
I can feel its cold behind my eyes,
can smell how many miles
it ran from the high snow
past deer and mountain quail.

I have to sit down for a minute
when I taste bear dung
in our water—it's the old male,
brown, dusty, back of Wellman Burn.

Our water has moved pebbles
shaped like hearts (I found one
in San Ysidro Creek), boulders,
whole mountains, shaped
the earth—taste it, taste it!

In my blue enameled cup, our water
is white as milk at first;
clearing, it whispers at the edges
of my mouth, runs in my neck
under my shirt, cool as a lizard.

Sometimes I go in the kitchen,
just to think about
our water; I have to sit down
and look out the window for a while,
watch the air opening the leaves.

My heart is beating like a stone.

It turns down the drain
with the turning earth, our water,
running away to rain.

CASTING A VOTE

In the eyes of the brown bear
back of Wellman Burn there is
a cloud, and I will clear
them, open deep in their retinas
my own vision;
he will see me walking the canyon,
holding myself tight
under the contracting gray sky—

poems in the eyes of old bears!
I think I will vote
for him for President or Senator,
to hear him growl in Congress,
cracking plaster in White House
walls, white dust drifting
slowly down on the President's desk!

I work up the canyon
looking for sign; two doe
rise from a thicket,
sailing without sound down
the dry meadows. A cloud
clears from my eye, sun burning
away dead scar tissue;
heat in the look opens mind.

Bear talk! pure harsh sound
walks water up creek, rock
by rock, to where I chew hard sausage,
a handful of nuts—he is voting
with his left front paw in water,
snapping the air, upwind.

November 1968

AIMING AT BIRDS

Hitting the keys in a bad time,
hours at my oak table,
staring into a mirror,
thinking about shaving—

even if you loved me,
you wouldn't today. Or,
counting my books, thinking
about being a potter

instead, going away somewhere
for a while, sitting
in some bar for hours—
there are too many possibilities,

none of them satisfactory.
There are too many poems
already, too many images,
none just what I wanted.

I think I will go
and lie down and try
not to think
and think so much—

lie under the trees, mumble,
scratch, spit—unshaven,
roll in the uncut grass,
dull and dirty as the earth.

The birds on the wires
stupid as words on a page;
I sling stones at them,
aiming to kill.

Eyes glittering at nothing
in their fragile skulls,
they murmur unintelligibly
but will not fly—

my arms ache trying
to get them up into air,
my eyes ache, my
fingers, the poem.

FIRST RAINS

In winter the rains begin,
flooding our drive
and blocking all the drains
with leaves and sticks;
a dead gopher, drowned, floats
in the lake under the car—

lists again! Wet leaves,
dead sticks, open blank eyes
of a stiff gopher, rains,
sticks—this is any good only
if I can get everything in:

the dripping live oak,
the hissing fire burning
cut brush, the powerful sky
building above the gray mountains,
the sow-bug
curling in my palm to a hard ball.

Such a poem could go on
and on, until . . .
                    Look,
look at things close,
they rage to the close eye,
intractable, stone-hard;

can they flame out into the air,
touching the skin of the world,
even the faintest touch?

The dead eyes of the gopher,
wet matted fur—its body
turns as I unplug the drains
with a shovel—
the cold brown water runs off,
speaking and muttering.

THE GARDEN

Six rows of pole beans grow
high above my head; I rain
on them, the arched stream of water,
cold from the green hose,
runs off silver in the dusk.

From top to top
the vines have grown across
each row, tangled arches
leading down to the live oak grove.

Owls plane three hundred yards
without a beat, then beat
once to settle in the swaying top
of a sycamore—six owls
tonight, flat-headed, white breasts
and underwings in the last sun
they catch at that height.
One Steller's jay patrols
my garden at dusk.

Crows call the night in
from the sea. The mountains
fall back flat, each ridge
going from gold to gray
by miles to the east.

From my cold right hand
I scatter drops of water
like a god. Leaves drink me;
a spider, black and yellow
in his web, tiptoes
to the center of his world
and stings a sacrifice to me.

The raccoon is waiting
in the brush to try the fence
around the new corn—
I see his tracks each morning
in the wet earth.

In my garden I am lonely
as a god; the animals sense
my fear and rustle nearer
in the dark. I tremble,
hear wind rising in the dark.

THE QUAIL

for Herbert W. Gottfried

The Algonquin local gods, or *manitous*, sometimes
"assume human proportions; but more frequently
they take the form of stones, which, being
broken, are found full of living blood and flesh."
Francis Parkman

I

The gray quail peck along our fence-line,
perky and quick; when the dogs range
along their noses into brambles
and under the pines eaten by red spiders,
the quail whirr everywhere at once.
They follow their piping into the air.

Two geldings gallop under the live oaks.
The bitch slinks under barbed wire
to chase the mule, who turns back suddenly,
head low, lips curled, and the dog
slides on its tail in wet clover.
I stoop to roll a stone into weeds;
it could cut tires in our rutted road.

Manitou, manitou of our sixteen acres,
the trees rustle high overhead
when you pass; you crack the mule's hoof.
Live oak bleeds red at the core,
and the eucalyptus breaks its branches
in the night—awake, I hear
the wild doves muttering on the wires.

II

In a stone, my blood lives
and beats in my ears; dark and thin,
my flesh feeds on itself—manitou
within, local god, break
open through my eyes! Like the quail,
I will rise up out of the cold ground,
singing; will dance on the soft earth.

Mulch of our bones, stone ground,
worked by red worms, turned with humus,
black dirt of the orange grove,
I put my boots lightly at angles
on your skin. Our world is a stone.

III

My Mexican friends—Johnny, Bebe,
Pedro, Chazzo, Uncle Bob—
bounce in the old truck
into the drive. They pop
the tops of beer cans
and flash their teeth
in the red tail-lights.

The truck bed is lined
with quail and rabbits;
spots of blood
shine on the stiff tarpaulin.
The truck radio
plays loud rock:

The Sunshine Company,
"Wondering why again."
Eric Burdon and the Animals.
The Stone Poneys: "I ain't sayin'
you ain't pretty, I'm just
sayin' I'm not ready. . . ."*
The Grateful Dead.

The quail, gray stones,
bleed slowly from their beaks;
the dogs whine at the tail-gate.
The cold of a beer can
noses up my arm, and we
laugh under the stars,
the Spanish moon. Indian faces
like gods with moustaches.

IV

The stones in the drive turn
under my feet, going back in,
and I lie in the dark—like
a root, it tightens itself to stones.

Are there many like me,
who will not crack? Who will
lie low, because we do not wish
to die? Who love with this grip

of the dark on our hearts?
When the whole begins
its necessary fracturing,
opening the earth along faults

* From "Different Drum," words and music by Michael Nesmit, © 1965,
1967 by Screen Gems-Columbia Music, Inc. Used by permission; reproduction prohibited.

to its living center,
shall we be there, singing
and dancing in the white fires?
How many know how we wish to open?

V

Manitou, manitou, god of stones,
god like a stone,
one day I threw a stone
and knocked a quail, warm gray
stone, to the cold ground.
Stunned, it lay in my hand
and prayed in its beating throat.
With a heart like a stone,
I broke its neck, and pushed
my knife against its breastbone.
Manitou, manitou, blood warm
as sun-bright stones spread
over my hand—light as gray
feathers, light as gray stone,
I rose over the earth,
over the orange grove, the stand
of live oaks, above the sycamore
and the ticking eucalyptus,
above the gray stone of myself,
and broke against the air.

One
All across America we came
this far to California—
here anything may grow.
Mornings the horses scratch
at the window screens, stretching
long necks over the stone wall.

Two
Married married married we
did it together!
Coast to coast by Volkswagen,
in love and anger, driving us
this far for seven years. Dear one,
we shall never do it again!

As I take your hand to help
you from the car, stiff from miles
we have come through, leaning
west for a week, I sense that you
sense three thousand miles
back of us. Our hands touch.

Three
Red tile roof, adobe, stone walls,
the horse pasture, the six horses,

a giant dog named Giant, a gray barn,
morning sun, late sun, the colors

touch us from light years away.
Black dirt around the orange trees.

Four

The man who owns the horses owns
a tractor with which he cuts
neat curves in the round earth

around our orange trees. Quail jump
whistling as he turns near nests.
We nest in bed till ten on Saturdays

listening to the tractor, orange
and black, thump and batter in the orchard.
We hear him shout, "Honey!"

to his blonde dog barking, barking.
I will squeeze forty-six small oranges
for one quart of breakfast juice.

Five

We think we know how to make love
in our new house with its red roof;
our bodies ache into color
from behind our eyes. If we touch
miles out into the sun we may grow.

Six

Here is how we eat oranges
in this state we are newcomers
to: first, walk twenty yards
out over the black plowed ground,

reach up and pull gently
at the trees—oranges will fall
into your paper sack soundlessly
as clouds butt islands

thirty blue miles out to sea.
Take the oranges behind the house,
sit on the low stone wall.
With your knife, blade

etched by acid like love,
cut off the top of an orange,
peel an inch-wide strip
around the cut. Open wide,

dear wife, and squeeze—
in this state (in which we shall
live forever) all one needs
to do is open wide,

and juice, hot from sun,
will fill your throat. Chuck
the pulp over your shoulder:
where it rots,
                anything may grow.

*Il fit un poëme et le commença
ainsi: "Muse, ne me dis rien!
Muse, tais-toi!"*
Jules Renard, Journal

II

MUTTERING

The night is as quiet as an empty bed,
an empty room.
I have white paint
around the edges of my fingernails;
last night we painted
the living-room. Tonight I lie
alone and edged
in white like a lie we have told
each other many years.
You—with the broken eardrum!
Listen to the empty night
lying next to you in a white bed.

*

If there are any dreams
she dreams that make no sense
to me she thinks less
of me—what can I do?

I have not felt her touch
alive, for some months.
She is going back into her dream,
leaving me behind.

She is dreaming of me,
as if I knew what she dreamt.

*

It is not your fault,
of course, or his, or his,
but mine, of course,
that he and you will laugh
together in your fine skins
at me, alone with my poems
again, of course. "So much
of his life goes by in suffering
which he must love more
than anything." Of course,
of course, of course, of course.

✳

He brings her incense to burn.
I love its smell,
and the solid thin line
of smoke that goes up straight
as string, then unravels
suddenly. She kisses him
outside, while I sit
cross-legged on the green rug,
in the half-dark,
watching the red coal
burn slowly down.

✳

Pretend the Dark

Because her eyes grow dark
behind their green, I cannot find
myself in them;
she shuts me out.
Pretend the dark means more

of her than I usually see,
or something better in her
that she will let me
find in her some day.
Go on, pretend. Pretend.

Or, that she does love me
when her hand does this, this,
across my skin.
Pretend her nails are
not quite possible as knives

slipping in as simply as
this line runs on to its end
and in. Let me write her
a poem—for her, I can do
anything at all. Pretend I will

*

This July one hundred tremors
shook the ground, all along
some fault in California—
cracked walls, windowpanes,
rocked me in my deck chair,
and scared the cats. Everywhere
the ground is shifting
beneath my feet. I can't sit still.
I leap and stamp, dancing
and pounding the ground.
I want the earth to shake again,
split all across America,
and all of us saved in the cracks.

*

This Week

First, she, well,
tells me she's having
an affair. Of course
I flip, and check

in with the shrink
again. On the way home,
stuffed with Librium,
I stop to watch

an old lady drown
on East Beach—
the pulmotor pumps
and hisses like a heart.

It was my birthday,
too. I remember
the Russians
invaded Czechoslovakia.

I come home to silence,
seven years of curses
in her eyes. Yes, I know,
life is holy, innocent,

terrible, pain and joy
ticking as one heart.
My father-in-law tells me:
"As one ages,

one begins to sense
the order of the universe,
how love governs
everything." God's heart,

humming everywhere,
like a bumblebee?
Ah, yes, yes—life
is holy, damned;

and they tell me
I'm not to blame!

*

I shall miss you, and not
ever live in the past again—
so much bad faith!

Now you hate my socks
and refuse to roll them up
after doing the laundry.

You hate my poison oak
which I got to anger you.

Now everything I do you don't
want me to do, and everything
I did you didn't want me to do.

Good-bye, good-bye!

You used to wear my socks
to bed when your feet were cold.

*

If silence is everywhere
it is because it is about time.
Altogether we talked
almost seven years; our marriage
license hid in a tin box,
listening and grimacing—
the only one of our important papers
to hear us.

The titles for the two cars,
the life insurance policies, the deed
to the old house on Capitol Hill,
my discharge, and the baby's
birth certificate, all fell
asleep at once.

But now, opening the tin box,
they rustle awake in our hands,
and we divide them among us—
this for you, that for me.
At the bottom, our marriage license,
fading and curling. Its last words:
"I gave you permission."

*

Our cat goes ten feet straight up
the stone wall—the two-toed bitch puppy
yaps after it, limps away
to sit down suddenly and dig a flea
from beneath its tail. Christ,
I'm sick of animals! What can they tell
me about myself—the goat
stuttering like my wife in a rage,
the horses rolling in the dust . . . ?

*

Balboa Island

After seven hours at the bar—
The Rolling Stones, the high edge
of pot at the back of my nose,
too many poets in one room—
I told you you were beautiful;
it was a discovery.

"You are like an Indian,
an India-Indian, beautiful,
just beautiful." And drunk,
I put cigarette ash on your forehead,
and you said, "I'm too wary,
too wary," and would not leave
with me, just yet.

Though later, while your son
sniffed in his bed, we were all-American
Indians on the convertible sofa,
whooping and scalping, painting
ourselves for war, passing
the peace pipe, and pulling feathers
from each other's hair. Early
the next morning the ash was smeared
along my cheek.

*

Biltmore Beach

On a cold gray day, I stand
beside my old car—cold, gray,
cold, gray, cold, blue,
blue, gray—the sea
is a music from which comes
the cold gray blue. . . .
That is not music.
Is there another human being
in the picture. Not yet.

She enters left. A girl
in a blue shirt,
whom I love instantly.
She throws her dog a red ball,
the sun fades in his mouth.
Do I love you, I ask her.

Not yet. The dog bounds
over gray rocks, bellowing
for the cold moon in her breast.
I get back in my gray car.
She raises her girlish arm
and waves good-bye. My old car
drives away on the blue road.

*

You hold the .22 pistol
in your hand, and think
of how the roof of your mouth
will blossom out
against the seats, the windows,
the white canvas top
of the old convertible,
and you think of your worth,
and your right to be loved,
and your responsibilities,
your strength and weakness,
and you think and think,
and where does it get you?
Not many can think that far.

*

Why do I suppose,
hearing the running
footsteps of any girl
behind me,
wherever it may be,
that she is running
after me?

*

Today I mailed letters to friends.
I forgot to put stamps on them,
and dropped them in the mailbox.
My friend the mailman will bring
them all back, and I will not dare
to send them out again.

*

I wept on the cold steps
of Holy Mother Church
at 4 A.M., drunk as Jesus
only knows on salty wine.

The priests called the cops,
the cops took me in,
and I knelt at the rail
of the booking-room
confessing everything:

I love Jesus, I love her,
I love you guys,
I am drunk and disorderly.

Open your cold doors then,
bless me with the clanging iron
and the turned key.

*

The bad dreams keep coming,
night after night.
Can it be all guilt?

Or is someone actually doing it to me?

First, the murder of my father
in his bed, and the red
blood eating calmly at the sheets.

Did I do it?

And the three homosexuals
drowned in the ornamental pool,
trapped against the wire drain,
in their white sneakers—

why did I hold up three fingers,
as if to make sure?

Then, feeding the pigeons
in the school yard, why did one fasten
his claws into my thumb,
pecking hard at the back of my hand?

I know I didn't do it, not
all by myself, not all of it.

*

Always I qualify the circumstances
under which I would wish to die—
today I wish to die only
if I would be born again.
Some promise me that I will
but I do not believe them.

My mother is naked and cold
as a statue; she struggles
to speak words she cannot think.
My father is naked as the dead;
no one is listening anymore.
Perhaps I can bring them to life
by dying, perhaps the world
would come alive if I died.

That would be something to hope for!

Now I will die, happily.
All my friends will celebrate,
drink wine, eat cheese and apples
in Oak Park, sing for my death.
My wife will kiss all the men,
if they are handsome—and they will be!
My daughter will leap about
like a kitten, my brother will shoot
his sergeant and come home.

The stone of my mother will crack
open, and waters will flow
into my father's grave. He will rise
up, and lift me in his arms,
and, when I am dead,
I will not believe I am dead.

*

I would like to write a poem
like a great hammer, beating
a huge sheet of black steel.
The Russians say, "It takes a hammer
of gold to open an iron door."
I must do everything myself,
it seems. Now I must write
poems like golden hammers.
Perhaps I shall open.
Must I do everything myself?
I do not hear any hammering.

*

Casting the *I Ching*, three coins
six times, American pennies—
heads or tails, odd or even,
yin or yang, building the hexagram;

old Calvinist from the heartland!
Shaking Abraham Lincoln
for the Book of Changes, saying
the Chinese syllables in California,

K'un, Tui, K'an, echoing
the Dutch heard in Wisconsin,
thinking of old things: lake,
water, stone, thorn and thistles,

the Judgment of Oppression,
the Image of Exhaustion,
the Lake above, the Water below,
a strong six in the third place:

"He enters his house
and does not see his wife."

TYPING

"When I type," you typed,
"the foot-long incision
on my belly itches."
You were always writing me
of plans for Caribbean cruises
to recuperate. "No sweat,"
you said, "they've cut nothing
out of me that matters.
Give me a bourbon to clear
my throat; they're painting
the apartment and the cat
is howling in an empty closet.
I can only work ten hours
a day to stay alive."

When I went to Providence
to see you, they wouldn't
let me see you. The rain fell
on the good and on the bad.
I lay on the hotel bed, hearing
whiskey in the old pipes,
and read over your letters—
like mine, on yellow paper
and filled with bad typing.

I listen to the nurse
on the telephone, trying to hear
you behind her soft voice:
I hear hums, the small gurgling
of tubes in your body,
soft voices murmuring in Dutch,
slow water in canals—

and the rattle of a typewriter,
all we knew of each other.

PART OF A WEEK IN WASHINGTON

On Tuesday we saw the varied thrush,
Mount Baker, and the gill-netters
frozen in the bay. Old Crow
in the coffee, we felt great.

Wednesday we woke with hangovers.
Stomachs growling, we fried eggs
in butter, our gal hollering
down the stairs, "You guys eat shit!"

Bob, the next day was Thursday
and the cops stopped us. Gifted
and determined, we plowed
your VW bus through weather

that only led to Friday. By then
the poets looked old and tired.
The thrush flew, Mount Baker floated
in a cloud. Bob, let's forget the rest.

SONG

Who is crying beak, beak, beak
in the swamp behind the big city
of homosexuals and police?
                       Querulous,
indecorous, smacking for seeds
that will grow inside like words,
filling your belly with long poems
of loss and the joke of love,

I hear you snapping back, back, back,

ah,
fucked duck, still singing, rattling
like the severed hand at the door,
weeping from stiff black eyes,
crying like a thumb twisted back hard.

MOOSE CALL

His voice comes
muffled as many miles
as we are from Fairbanks

through cold from
Alaska where footprints
freeze deep all

the years he speaks . . .
whispering south, forever.
Now we cannot live

easily on white beaches,
among creaking palms,
ice-plant. We follow

the frost-ringed steps
into his throat, into
cold within the dark skull.

OLD COUNTRY

My father! My mother!
I see that you are dying.
I am a cruel son.

Behind you, tall shapes
edge up from the ground,
trees, smoke, spirits.

In pictures, in my mind,
Holland is water—
the canals, the sea

rising behind the dikes,
the small lakes
which are ponds, glowing

behind the stone cottages.
I see water standing
in your aging eyes.

The turning shadows
of old windmills stir
the gray water. No,

in the low lands,
from behind dusty lindens,
I am a dark shape

rising behind you.
This is a message from
an old country.

How can I comfort you?

CHARMING THE MOON

At the ford, while grass-green frogs
continue and continue their high singing,

we crush wild fennel in our hands, a charm
to keep the magic going strong. Well,

we are animals, we say, and our children
are animals, and we will all survive.

The water in the creek runs silver, quick,
upstream to the moon, and down the canyon

to the sea, through rocks, moss, past frogs.
Everywhere the evidence of continuing:

under the pavement sow-bugs, white grubs,
slick tendrils drill; through trees,

sycamore, live oak, the quarter moon
is rising, falling, appearing, disappearing,

around each curve of Mountain Drive.
An opossum, round shadow, wavers in shadow.

We will survive. The moon will draw back
softly at the touch of the astronaut's foot,

and with wild fennel we'll charm it right
again, for all us animals, and green frogs

at the ford. Here's the real moon, in cupped
hands in the water. Drink, children, sing.

THE BEAD COLORS

I wear the beads you made me
it is very late
the colors begin to tell me
where we find ourselves

bright red for the slow-turning
patrol car blinker, the siren
just dead, and heavy silence
waiting in the streets

the white beads are helmets
of motorcycle riders
white bandages, white ash
white roads in the Mojave

yellow and orange say
your wife and child
are all light
yellow and orange wait
glowing like California poppies

and the deep red is blood
Michael, of which there is much
the deep red stain
seeping through the fatigue shirt
and the black shirt
and all the maps

the blue beads are a sea
between us; the sea is alive
and we shall cross it
we will become the sea
we will move up and down
like tides, touching everywhere

green is in your eyes
and in my eyes
soft jade on the beaches
the winter mountains
lemon leaves and the money
which is no longer any good to us

brown beads, square wooden
beads, the colors of the earth
many now hate
the brown dust of Mono Camp
the red and gray browns
of eucalyptus, the brown
water at the hot springs

it is very late, it is dark
beyond the glow of colors
the beads speak
they say resist, they say
friend find peace

AMERICA

All of us are writing poems
about you, as if you were
a friend, another poet,
a beautiful woman,
or a country in which we live.

At times, like a beautiful
lover, you take away all
our energy. Each day
as slow as street tar.
Like a beautiful woman,
you excite us, and we pace
through all the rooms.

You are a friend who calls
long distance
when he's in trouble
for hitting a cop.
Sometimes we drive
four hours at night
to try to be with you.

We can't write without you.
We are writing about you
all the time. Your words
mean so much to us.
We write down everything you say.

Like a friend, a poet,
a beautiful woman,
you are a country
in which we live every day.

Open is broken.
  Norman O. Brown, *Love's Body*

IV

MIX

Take her hand
and lead her
inside the room,

1. A large light room, on the second floor of a red brick mansion. A bedroom with an ornate old-fashioned bed. A maid enters, walks to the closet, opens the door. Mason jars filled with clear water are stacked inside.

Morning
raga;
glass
splintering,

put your arms
around her,
your face in
her hair;
whisper in
Spanish.
See her bright
eyes!
She begins to
unbutton your
blue chambray
shirt,
her hands
very warm
on your chest;

2. Four table model FM radios on four small white tables, each in a spotlight. They burst into flame.

coughing,

3. Steps on concrete pavement, building in volume, coming nearer. They stop. Striking match. Running water. Far off, a motorcycle. The steps continue.

slow, heavy
breathing,

4. An old man threads his way from left to right through a maze of pipe scaffolding.

an airplane;

the bed seems
to grow larger
and larger;

5. Close-up of large rock, which becomes the forehead of my friend Michael, which becomes an aerial view of southern California, which becomes the inside of a baby's mouth.

wind creaking
in the
eucalyptus,

6. On your bedroom wall an Indian is scalping a child; extreme close-up of blood welling in drops from child's skull. The Indian rips off the scalp. A knock at your window.

sound of
your weeping,

finally you lie
down with her
to make love
to her,

7. A man and woman speak rapidly and at the same time, very loudly, in Spanish. We learned Spanish in high school together.

small cries
of love;

8. While you and I are making love, the sound of afternoon television drowns out your small cries.

camera click-
ing and
whirring,

in this noisy
world.

9. I play a tape of my daughter singing while I am taking her picture. You call to me in Spanish on the radio.

a knock at
your
window,

Quietly,
quietly.

10. I reach from the screen to
    switch off the recorder; in the
    background miles of Mason jars,
    each filled with a shoe. We hold
    hands. Weeping. Steps. A car
    starts, leaves. War whoops,
    hooves. The film runs off the
    reel with a clatter. Static.
    Test pattern.

silence.

HERE ARE THE WORDS

Here are the gray mountains
silhouetted against the gray-blue sky;
here is the electric guitar
flashing in the baby spotlights;

here is the great fish washed up
on the broad white beaches of California;
here is the child born
without a father or mother at home;

here, love, is the huge sound
of the neighbor's stereo through the wall;
here is the thin edgy taste
of marijuana in the flower-filled air;

here is the ornamental pool
neglected and full of green floating scum;
here is the raven crying
in the high top of the creek sycamore;

here is the gray sky guitar baby
the fish white born father or mother,
here is the huge wall edgy air,
here is the ornamental green crying creek;

here, my love, my present love,
are all the words I find tonight
to fill the silence in which I write,
a ceremony of riven connections:

take mountains, electric, blue, the
flashing, fish, California, child, home,
the sound neighbors, the thin flowers,
the ornamental scum, the raven sycamore,

for it is all I have to give you,
and we must believe it is enough.

ROCK AND SEA

Walking Toward the Sea

I

And under such a sky,
such a sky as large as this is, as
deafening,
            in the midst of our joy
at being together under it,
down settles such deep loss
that I lie down, lie down in the grass,
            on the beckoning ground,
and watch myself walk on with you,
going on
(which I do not understand) hand
                        in hand.

II

My fear—how shall I learn from it?
Contain it? Correctly gauge
its intentions, how it wishes
to contain my life, setting boundaries
to experience, to love,
to our love?—
            since I fear you,
I fear others, fear myself,
begin from there: given limits,
I begin the definition, and the name
of love,
            the verse, the line,
driving back, holding, opening,
extending as the line extends to its end,
where I fear nothing,
                        not the strange sea
opening before us,
which we have not felt before.

A *Strong Tide*

I sailed many days
beyond sight of land in a small **boat**.
When the horizon darkened
I could feel land rising again—
channel fever—
and when I landed I felt you.
familiar to my hands
as water, the pulse of salt blood.
There is an ocean in your arm,
a strong tide!

Too easy.
It was just a remark.
You said, too earnestly,
your ear against your wrist,
"I feel an ocean in my arm."
You wanted to be in love

with a poet! I try to make
language become you, me,
our love, a specific moment
in a motel near the sea.
There is a strong tide tonight.

There is no ocean in your arm.
The ocean is hissing out there.
Steadily, like the blood in your arm.
I smell the salt.
We sail away.

East Beach

The cold gray blue sea
warms, brightens at all
its moving edges with gold
and diamond-white discs—

raising an arm from water
brings the sun to your hand,
shaking your hair from your eyes
creates thousands of new planets.

When we stand in shallows
salt water runs down our legs,
the birds clash around us
with high cries in the huge air.

Whatever love does it does
suddenly in this fallacious world.
We are not mistaken; the warm sea
is there every day we come to it.

Riding by the Sea

The horses go sideways,
edging for home;
we kick back, forcing
them to water.

Their hooves click
on stones,
then sink deep
into wet sand;

obsessively,
the beach goes on
forever.
Perhaps that frightens

horses.
We say, how did it
begin, how will
it all end?

Lean forward now,
walk the horses
up the cliff trails
to the meadow.

California poppies
fall away
from hooves.
Below, the sea opens.

Strange sea.
Open. Shut. Open.
Two turns
of the reins

around the limb
of a fallen eucalyptus.
The horses stay,
looking back.

Fewer and fewer
words for it.
Just what it is.
Spit on a stone

to see the mica
sparkle.
Stone like an egg.
The fragility

of what we are,
where we are, together.
Mount, let horses
take us home.

Lean back, down
sea cliffs.
Stone in my fist;
finding the way.

Let it drop
at the water's edge.
Found once,
I'll find it again.

Rock and Sea

The sea breaks rocks,
opens them to sun,
and many voices speak
along the beaches—

tides pull many words
into the sea.
In rock the silence
waits for water.

The sea breaks rocks
to speak; hear the whisper
to the sea to rise!
Hear the sea name love!

Many voices wait
within the rock, unheard.
Words ache within
the veins of rock.

This rock in my hand
has many names.
I feel the sea listen,
and begin to rise.

Rocks wait in love,
sea rises toward love.
What are our names?
Rock and sea, love.

TRYING TO COME APART
Notes for a novel

Get it over with: new poems or none at all.
None at all. Why are there no poems like fly-casting?
Who is building a poem stone by stone
like a viaduct? All I see are poems that drip,
drip, drip, drip; our poems follow us
like drops of blood on the trail.
We are looking for a deep bush in which to hide
from Indians, bloodhounds,
bounty-hunters.
                              Keep going.
Write a novel that is finally silent,
that is a deep well of silence, write a poem
that begins in the middle and goes out
in all directions, or a short poem
that takes years and years to read, or
a book-length poem that can be read at a glance.

Trying to come apart is how to get it together.
Write a novel about a poet. Write poems
for the poet in the novel. Write the novel
the poet wishes to write. Write what you know best.
Write silence.
                              Keep writing.
Trying to come apart is how to come together.

It is about silence, it is not easy, it is
drifting away, it is about time: one moment
there is silence, then there is a sound.
There are many sounds in the wilderness, and
suddenly there is one sound. The snake
scratches leaves. Think of a bear.
There is a snatch of his hair on a creeper.
Black Lake is still, then it is moving.
Write silence, stop time.

There is only stone and water;
moving and not moving; stasis and motion.
The still point . . . the dancer
and the dance. . . . Every day
there is a moment when one has to take it
all apart and put it back together.
Prose. Cut it anywhere along the line
and it is prose again.
                            Writing is always
lists: a stick of blue incense, my watch,
a mat knife, a rough pot, stacks
of old poems, a stone, the sea,
a book, your thin fingers. Everyone
I love.

Things simply happen. The news
on the radio. The center holds,
but where is it? Life is not worth
living. Can you imagine the existence
of anything that cannot be named?
I am trying to prove I love you.
Its name is that-which-cannot-be-named.
Things simply happen, happen, happen.
Small blocks of black ink on the page.

A stone like a heart, a gray quail,
the sow bug, a tin box, an iron door,
the warm sea, a strong tide, our own water—

go on, and on, and on, and out, and

poems that are signs, are scars. Broken
leaf. Bent twig.
                    Write it.
All. Trying to come apart is coming
together is love is writing; write what
you know least; write toward silence;
write toward the end; write trying
to come apart. Come apart. Stop writing.
                    do not stop
Come down the trail to the last camp
and the sound of typing. I have split rock
and found blood, and words,
                    and gone into the sea,
                    the strange sea, for silence.

I am afraid to come apart. I am trying
to come apart. I am coming
together

Pitt Poetry Series

James DenBoer, *Learning the Way*
 (1967 U.S. Award of the International Poetry Forum)
James DenBoer, *Trying to Come Apart*
Jon Anderson, *Looking for Jonathan*
Jon Anderson, *Death & Friends*
John Engels, *The Homer Mitchell Place*
Samuel Hazo, *Blood Rights*
David P. Young, *Sweating Out the Winter*
 (1968 U.S. Award of the International Poetry Forum)
Fazıl Hüsnü Dağlarca, *Selected Poems*
 (Turkish Award of the International Poetry Forum)
Jack Anderson, *The Invention of New Jersey*
Gary Gildner, *First Practice*
David Steingass, *Body Compass*
Shirley Kaufman, *The Floor Keeps Turning*
 (1969 U.S. Award of the International Poetry Forum)
Michael S. Harper, *Dear John, Dear Coltrane*
Ed Roberson, *When Thy King Is A Boy*
Gerald W. Barrax, *Another Kind of Rain*
Abbie Huston Evans, *Collected Poems*
Richard Shelton, *The Tattooed Desert*
 (1970 U.S. Award of the International Poetry Forum)
Adonis, *The Blood of Adonis*
 (Syria-Lebanon Award of the International Poetry Forum)

The poems in this book are set in Linotype Electra, duplexed here with the cursive rather than the italic. The composition and printing are the work of Heritage Printers, Inc. and the binding was done by Nicholstone Book Bindery. The design is by Gary Gore.